Bibliographical Series
of Supplements to 'British Book News'
on Writers and Their Work

GENERAL EDITOR
Bonamy Dobrée

FRANCIS THOMPSON
from a chalk drawing of 1907 in by Neville Lytton
the National Portrait Gallery

FRANCIS THOMPSON

by

PETER BUTTER

PUBLISHED FOR

THE BRITISH COUNCIL

and the NATIONAL BOOK LEAGUE

by LONGMANS, GREEN & CO.

LONGMANS, GREEN & CO. LTD.
48 Grosvenor Street, London W.1
Thibault House, Thibault Square, Cape Town
605–611 Lonsdale Street, Melbourne C.1

LONGMANS, GREEN & CO. INC.
119 West 40th Street, New York 18

LONGMANS, GREEN & CO.
20 Cranfield Road, Toronto 16

ORIENT LONGMANS LTD.
Calcutta   Bombay   Madras
Delhi   Hydrabad   Dacca

First Published in 1961
© Peter Butter 1961

Printed in Great Britain by
F. Mildner & Sons, London, E.C.1

CONTENTS

ACKNOWLEDGEMENTS

I am grateful to the late Mrs. Dallyn (Viola Meynell) and to Mrs. Sowerby (Olivia Meynell) for allowing me to see and to quote from the Thompson MSS in their possession; and to the editor of *A Review of English Literature* for permission to reproduce in substance parts of an article that appeared in the January 1961 number.

¶ FRANCIS THOMPSON was born on 16 December 1859 at Preston, Lancashire. He died in London on 13 November 1907.

FRANCIS THOMPSON

I: INTRODUCTION

WHEN Francis Thompson's first volume, *Poems*, appeared in 1893 Tennyson and Browning were dead, Alfred Austin was poet Laureate, the Rhymers' Club were meeting at the Cheshire Cheese and were producing, in general, rather pale and world-weary verses. It was the era of *The Yellow Book*, when the predominant mood among writers was desire to escape from the ugliness and materialism of the time. Thompson, once a silent guest at the Rhymers' Club, was also a refugee from the nineteenth century, but his verses were neither pale nor world-weary; they were highly coloured and sought to express a positive vision of a realm of spiritual realities rather than a rejection of the world of every day. A few thought they found in him true splendour and profound vision; but others thought the splendour merely one of rags and patches, the vision the product of drugs and dreams, of the sentimental reveries of one too weak to deal with the real world. His circle of enthusiastic admirers grew, however, and the collected edition of 1913 had a remarkably good sale; since then he has held the allegiance of a considerable number of ordinary readers of poetry, but the critics have remained, predominantly, hostile. Every one agrees that there are some fine things in his work, but he is blamed for over-ornate diction, imprecise and pretentious imagery, lack of form, derivativeness and pseudo-profundity. If the severer critics are right, we may safely ignore all but a few anthology pieces; but we ought to take a close look at him before deciding that they are so. For it may be that he possesses qualities that are all the more valuable to us for being unfashionable. The most admired work of the younger poets today is precise, controlled, intelligent, but rather lacking in fire and in range and depth of vision. These poets are, admirably, intent upon being honest, on not saying more than they have really felt and known to be true—and this often means that they do not say very much. In contrast Thompson comes to us as the Bard, claiming inspiration, claiming to reveal a vision of the kingdom of God to be found 'in no strange land', but all around us; for, though humble about himself, he was confident of his vision—'this my seeing is not weak'. This confidence gives his work an exhilarating quality rare in modern poetry. The doubt remains, however, to what extent he succeeded in adequately embodying his vision in words.

II: LIFE

Something of the same doubt exists about the man as about the poet. To what extent was he a truly religious seer, to what extent merely a neurotic dreamer?

He was born in 1859, the son of a Lancashire doctor; both his parents were Roman Catholic converts, and seem to have been kind and deeply religious people. He was a dreamy, unpractical gentle child, and from early days a great reader. Even in childhood he was rather a solitary, living in a realm of thoughts and imaginings which he could not, or would not, convey to others. He wrote of himself: 'There is a sense in which I have always been and even now remain a child. But in another sense I never was a child, never shared children's thoughts, ways, tastes, manner of life, and outlook on life. I played, but my sport was solitary sport, even when I played with my sisters; from the time I began to read (about my sixth year) the game often (I think) meant one thing to me and another (quite another) to them—my side of the game was part of a dream-scheme invisible to them. And from boys, with their hard practical objectivity of play, I was tenfold wider apart than from girls with their partial capacity and habit of make-believe.' A solitary, but at the same time affectionate —that is one of the paradoxes of his life. In a late note-book he wrote of the 'desolation and terror of, for the first time, realizing that the mother can lose you, or you her, and your own abysmal loneliness and helplessness without her', and compared this feeling to that of first fearing oneself to be without God.

He did not want to grow up. His time at school—from 1870 to 1877 at Ushaw College near Durham—did something, but not much, to take him out of himself. He began to write there—not only serious verse and prose, but also humorous verses which were much admired; and the liturgical life of the seminary must have had an effect upon him; but he seems to have made no close friends. He attracted the affectionate interest of the masters, but was considered too unpractical and absent-minded to be acceptable for the priesthood, for which he had been intended. This was the first great disappointment of his life; his sense of failure over this tended to throw him yet further in upon himself.

The next ten years were, outwardly at least, a time of uninterrupted failure. For the first six he was a medical student; but he disliked and neglected his studies, not being able to stand the sight of blood. At about the age of twenty he fell ill and began to take opium (then still freely prescribed by doctors, and easily obtainable), perhaps influenced by the gift from his mother, shortly before her death in 1880, of *The Confessions of an English Opium Eater* by De Quincey, to whose character and situation then and later his own were in some ways remarkably similar. When it became clear that he would never pass his medical examinations, various other openings were tried for him, but in vain. In 1885, after a painful interview with his father, whom he was never able to take into his confidence and who, he later insisted, was in no way to blame, he departed abruptly for London—apparently with no particular object or hope. At first his father sent a small allowance, but after a time he stopped collecting it. He was befriended, and given work, by a kindly bootmaker, but would settle to no regular employment. He fiercely defended the privacy of the intense inner life which he was to be able to reveal only in his writing. Instinctively he knew what were not the right paths for him, but did not yet know what was. So he became a down-and-out on the streets—sleeping in a shelter on the Embankment or even in the open air, picking up a precarious living by selling matches or unloading trunks from cabs or by other casual expedients, often spending what he earned on opium to dull the pain of his already disease-racked body, too ragged to dare even to go into a public library to read. He would have drifted to a useless and unnecessary death if help of just the right kind had not come in time.

In 1888 a poem he had sent to the Catholic literary monthly, *Merry England*, was published, and soon afterwards he arrived at the office of the editor, Wilfred Meynell—to all appearance a ragged, dirty, diseased tramp. Meynell displayed extraordinary goodness and patience in giving him not only immediate practical help, but friendship, respect and admiration, and in continuing to give these things for the next nineteen years. Thompson was persuaded, not without difficulty, to go to a hospital, was in part restored to health, and conquered for a time the opium habit. Release from opium and contact with people who appreciated him set free the vein of poetry which had lain hidden under his diffidence and which flowed strongly for the next seven years, 1889-96, and then almost dried up.

After his rescue he remained the same wayward, incompetent, gentle creature as before, and his life continued to be in some ways a sad, solitary and painful one. From 1889 to 1890 he stayed with a community of Franciscan monks in Sussex, and from 1892-96 he was most of the time near another Franciscan community in Wales. At other times he lived a nomadic life in various London lodgings, constant visits to the large Meynell family giving him the nearest to a home that he was to know. He was often ill and in pain and at such times tended, especially towards the end of his life, to relapse into taking opium. In a distant and adoring way he was in love with Alice Meynell, and was briefly attracted by Katherine King, a vivacious and intelligent girl he met in London, and by Maggie Brien, with whose family he lodged in Wales; but none of these affairs went, outwardly, beyond shy affection, and he was to remain always on the fringe of the ordinary human community. Nevertheless the few who knew him well sensed a serenity, even gaiety, in him, and felt that he was some one to be admired more than pitied. During his last ten years he made his living as a reviewer for literary periodicals, writing a large number of articles of a very high and consistent standard. In 1907 he died of tuberculosis at the age of forty seven.

Not having faced his difficulties it is not for us to pass judgement on Thompson the man; but our attitude towards him will make some difference to the way in which we approach his poetry. It is sentimental to deny his weaknesses. His sufferings—physical (illness and privation), mental (loneliness, etc.) and spiritual (consciousness of his failings)—were to a large extent self-induced. His withdrawn temperament led him to opium, which increased his isolation and sapped his will power. He constantly sought to escape from the responsibilities of adult life; hence arose his inconsiderate behaviour to his parents and others, his choosing of women to love who could not return his love and so make a claim on him, his unpunctuality, his self-pity. His religion did not enable him to live a disciplined life, nor lead to the performance of many practical acts of charity. This is part of the truth, but not the whole. His notebooks reveal a constant struggle to conform his life to what he knew his religion demanded. All who knew him well found him a gentle and loveable person, whose sweetness of character had been quite unstained by his three years on the London streets. Those to whom he could reveal himself admired his intelligence and spiritual insight. Coventry Patmore, a fierce, outwardly haughty and intolerant old man, of whom young poets were justifiably in awe, had, Katherine Tynan records, 'an enormous opinion of Francis Thompson. He would talk to few people and listen to few people; but he would talk and listen to Francis Thompson by the hour'.

On the surface it may seem that Thompson just drifted through life—first carried down stream to beggary and near death, then saved by Meynell and allowing his life to be organised for him; but at deeper—emotional and spiritual—levels he showed great toughness. One sees this by comparing him to some of the minor poets of the nineties, such as Dowson. He wrote in a notebook of Dowson: 'A frail and (in an artistic sense) faint minor poet . . . The major poet moulds, rather than is moulded by, his environment.' Out of the sad life of Dowson came only some palely beautiful cries of pain; but Thompson was able, at his best, to rise above his suffering and use it. If he had really been a drifter, what bitter and sordid fruit might have been expected as the product of the environment of much of his life—pain, loneliness, the London streets and the characters he met there? The product in fact was a considerable body of verse, expressing a joyous vision, not of the sordid, but of the Kingdom of God seen all around him in people and in nature; a large quantity of very intelligent and well-written prose; and his own unembittered and gentle character. Some purpose after all was served by those apparently wasted years.

Given his temperament and other difficulties, it may well be that his life should be regarded as a triumph. Nevertheless, the truly religious man in him, and the true artist in him, never wholly overcame the dreamer and escapist.

III: POETRY

I will first briefly survey the range of Thompson's poetry; then have a closer look at a few poems; and finally consider his use of words.

(i) Survey

The poems can be roughly classified, as to content, into those which deal with (a) people, (b) nature, (c) poetry and (d) religion. Of course, nearly all of them are in a broad sense religious, but we can distinguish those which deal more directly with man's relationship to God from those which approach Him through people, nature and poetry.

(a) The first category includes poems connected with Alice Meynell (the two series *Love in Dian's Lap* and *Ultima* and a few others), with Katie King (the *Ad Amicam* sonnets, etc.) and with Maggie Brien (*A Narrow Vessel*), and poems addressed to children. It is typical of Thompson (perhaps of poets in general) that these poems celebrate relationships in which the current of feeling was checked in real life, was able to flow freely only in poetry. Alice Meynell was able to be his muse, the inspirer of poetry, all the better for being safely inaccessible. These poems cover rather a narrow range of emotions. They tell us little about human behaviour, or the day to day changes of human relationships. The people mentioned are present only in a shadowy way. There is little description—of what they did, of what they looked like, or even, in a precise way, of their characters. Thompson is concerned not with them, but with his own emotions, his own insights. (Does not love poetry tend, paradoxically, to be very egocentric?) If we want to know social life or the more superficial levels of feeling we must turn to a man of wider experience like Byron. Thompson claims to give us something different—an insight into the nature of love and into the relationship of human to divine love. Together the poems make up a spiritual autobiography. His love is checked, restricted; he feels isolated, and succumbs for a time to self-pity; then works through self-pity to acceptance; then is able to see the very checks themselves as a grace, because they have enabled him to see beyond merely natural love to that to which natural love should lead. He sums it up in a notebook: 'The function of natural love is to create a craving which it cannot satisfy. And then only has its water been tasted in perfect purity, if it awakens an insatiate thirst for wine.' A woman loved can be a Jacob's ladder leading towards God. Human love is an emblem of, and preparation for, the union of the soul with God. The poems contain not only passionate feeling, but also quite clear and precise ideas as to the nature and function of love. Only intermittently does the expression rise to the height of the theme, but several of the poems contain touches at least of greatness, for instance *Before her Portrait in Youth*, *Manus Animam Pinxit*, *Love Declared*, *Grace of the Way*, *Arab Love Song* and *A Fallen Yew*. Collectively Thompson's love poetry is, for me, more valuable than the more perfect works of others who deal with the more superficial and obvious levels of experience; it widens horizons.

(b) As a nature poet also Thompson has little to tell us of the surface appearance of things. He is capable of the occasional vivid descriptive line (e.g., 'Green spray showers lightly down the cascade of the larch') and of evoking the atmosphere of a scene (e.g., of London the night before the Diamond Jubilee: 'Night; and the street a corpse beneath the moon, Upon the threshold of the jubilant day'); but these are not the things at which he especially excels. He is not concerned to describe the surface of things, but to express an imaginative vision of all things as alive, as connected, and as the art of God. The landscape of his poems is a strange and violent one. Suns die weltering in their blood, stars are blown to a flare by great winds or are puffed out by the Morning Hours; large cosmic forces are handled with a sometimes too easy assurance which tends to trivialise them. But even the less good poems (even the, in parts absurd, *Corymbus for Autumn*, for example) have a Dionysian energy and joy behind them which most modern poems, with all their intelligence and control, lack.

They convey a vision of things rather similar to Van Gogh's, another neurotic who was also a true visionary and a true, if imperfect, artist. One of the best nature poems is

Contemplation, which reveals a pattern of energy within calm existing in nature, in the spiritual life and in the life of the artist. It begins with a description of a beautiful natural scene on a bright morning after a shower; everything seems to be quiet and at rest:

> The river has not any care
> The passionless water to the sea to bear;
> The leaves have brown content;
> The wall to me has freshness like a scent
> And takes half-animate the air,
> Making one life with its green moss and stain . . .

Underneath the stillness great energies are present. This state is compared to that of the soul in contemplation, and especially to that of the poet's mind when, calm and receptive, it is really at its most creative:

> No hill can idler be than I;
> No stone its inter-particled vibration
> Investeth with a stiller lie . . .

In poets, as in skies, 'lurk un-tumultuous vortices of power'. In writing of the 'inter-particled vibration' within the apparent stillness of the stone Thompson shows a capacity, which is rather rare, to assimilate scientific knowledge into poetry. Elsewhere he writes of the 'shy universes' unseen by normal eyesight, but revealed by the microscope, through which one sees:

> The dusted anther's globe of spiky stars . . .
> And every water-drop a-sting with writhing wars . . .

and of the vital activity within the insignificant-looking green scale which is the prothallus of the fern and which contains within itself the two sexes.

Thompson is, perhaps, at his most effective not when handling in a rather facile way sun, moon, stars, great winds, etc., but when showing great things in small:

> I do not need the skies'
> Pomp when I would be wise . . .

> One grass blade in its veins
> Wisdom's whole flood contains . . .

(if one is able to see in it)

> God focussed to a point.

For him:

> Nature is whole in her least things expressed,
> Nor know we with what scope God builds the worm.

Nature, for him, is the art of God and expresses, even in small things, something of His nature. But he is not, like many nineteenth century poets, sentimental about her. Many of his contemporaries, turning from their sorrows in the world of men, sought to lay their heads in the lap of mother Nature and to find there some response, some tenderness; even to find in her a guide, a teacher. Thompson replies that if one imagines that one hears any response from the great heart of nature to one's longing for sympathy, it is only the echo of one's own heart-beat that one hears.

> Lo, here stand I and Nature, gaze to gaze,
> And I the greater.

Nature 'nor gives nor teaches'; she 'has no hands to bless', and has no use for the obeisance of man.

(c) A considerable proportion of Thompson's poetry is concerned with his own experience as a poet. One sometimes gets impatient with his self-consciousness (typical of him, and of modern poets in general); but in a few passages (e.g., in parts of *Sister Songs*, in *Contemplation*, *From the Night of Forebeing* and *The Cloud's Swan Song*) he does succeed in conveying powerfully something of what it feels like to be a poet, and he has interesting things to say about the nature of poetic inspiration:

> The poet is not lord
> Of the next syllable may come . . .

What he plans today may turn out differently tomorrow.
Vision cannot be commanded, will not become his mate
'by law and vow', but:

> Disguised in life's most hodden-grey,
> By the most beaten road of everyday
> She waits him, unsuspected and unknown.

To a poet a Dream may come:

> And suddenly his limbs entwine,
> And draw him down through rock as sea-nymphs
>   might through brine.

Into the depths of his own self, perhaps; and, possibly, the
Dream is something rising out of the depths of his own
mind. But it does not seem like that; the Dream, the vision,
seems to be something coming to him from the outside and
taking hold of him; and so it is spoken of as another being,
with whom he can—is forced to—have relations. The
moment passes, and the work of art that is born from it
can never be a complete embodiment of it.

What is the significance of the vision which meets the
poet unexpectedly on life's road? Is it simply a release of
energy from the depths of the self? Is the belief in inspiration
an illusion? Thompson would deny it. In a state of calm and
receptiveness, he says, the poet is able to become a vehicle:

> His heart's a drop-well of tranquillity;
> His mind more still is than the limbs of fear,
> And yet its unperturbed velocity
> The spirit of the simoom mocks.
> He round the solemn centre of his soul
> Wheels like a dervish, while his being is
> Streamed with the set of the world's harmonies.

The strong images used here are not mere flourishes; they
are seriously intended. He wrote in a review: 'The insight

of the poet springs from intuition, which is the highest reason, and is acquired through contemplation, which is the highest effort.' By his use of the word contemplation he deliberately links the activity of the poet to that of the mystic. 'The weapon of the poet or saint is intuition, and contemplation is the state, the attitude, which disposes the mind to receive intuitions.' By contemplation the poet makes his mind still, and in this state is able to receive intuitions which are not mere whimsies created by his imagination, but perceptions given to it. By linking poet and saint he does not, of course, imply that the poet is necessarily, in his life, a saintly man; but he does seriously mean that a kind of submission, a kind of fidelity (an absolute honesty, a fidelity to his own experience, his own vision), is required of the poet which is parallel to that required of the mystic. He was well aware of the dangers of false mysticism, and of the possibility of its being confused with the true. False mysticism is mere emotionalism, whereas true mysticism is insight reached by contemplation, and is not contrary to reason. There is the same kind of difference between the undisciplined outpourings of the sentimental writer and the work of the true poet, and the same kind of criteria can be used to distinguish false from true in the two realms. In both realms the condition in which true intuitions can be received is reached by discipline, by a self-naughting which clears the sight of the distortions of personal desire. The greatest art may start from a personal dilemma, but reaches beyond it; it can stand up to the scrutiny of reason, though again it goes beyond it.

It would take us too far to argue here whether Thompson's view of the nature of inspiration is true. It can, perhaps, be agreed that there is on the one side a state of slack day-dreaming which produces work of a sentimental and derivative kind, and on the other a state of receptiveness reached by discipline and concentrated effort which is quite different and produces work of a quite different kind—work which is at once intensely personal and something more than that. Some of Thompson's own work is dreamy and derivative—*Dream-Tryst*, for example, and *Absence;* these poems are less than personal. But usually he writes in a way which is unmistakably and distinctively his own, though many of his poems are no more than personal, being weighed down with his own sorrows. Sometimes, however, he rises to that mixture of passion and calm which is characteristic of major poetry.

(d) In his religious poems he tried, with varying success, to reach beyond absorption with his own sorrows to a state of calm and acceptance. He wrote in a notebook: 'The core of mysticism is a *fact*, not an understanding or a feeling. Still less is it an *endeavour* after a something nameless and unattainable. All true mystics know well about what they seek; and that it can be gained or missed according to the fidelity of their own effort. The thing sought is the *Union*.' In another notebook: 'A mystic poet who is vaporous fancy will not go far. Every such poet should be able to give a clear and logical prose resumé of his teaching as terse as a page of scholastic philosophy.' One could give such a resumé of the content of Thompson's religious poems, and show that what he had to say is in accordance with what the great adepts of the spiritual life have taught. That would not, of course, prove the poems to be good as poems—the quality of the emotion and the adequacy of the expression vary greatly; but it would show that such epithets as 'vague, cloudy, vaporous' apply much *less* to his than to most nineteenth century religious poems.

He believed himself to have been given unusual insight into spiritual facts, but was well aware of the inadequacy of the response he had made in life to his vision:

> 'Friend, whereto art thou come?' Thus Verity;
> Of each that to the world's sad Olivet
> Comes with no multitude, but alone by night,
> Lit with the one torch of his lifted soul,
> Seeking her that he may lay hands on her;
> Thus: and waits answer from the mouth of deed.

Knowing the insufficiency of his answer from the mouth
of deed he was afraid lest he might be among those who,
like Judas, had taken the immortal kiss of Truth and then
betrayed it—or rather, betrayed himself—and so earned
with Judas a guerdon of despair.

The Dread of Height well conveys a sense of the mixture
of joy and fear with which he visited the high places of the
spiritual life. He has drunk 'the drink which is divine', has
heard:

> . . . secret music, sweetest music
> From distances of distance drifting its lone flight

and yet, when he has victoriously climbed to the high place:

> My soul with anguish and recoil
> Doth like a city in an earthquake rock,
> As at my feet the abyss is cloven then,
> With deeper menace than to other men,
> Of my potential cousinship with mire.

He has been shown more than most men—so much the
greater his danger of falling, and his guilt if he does so.
The sense of awe which these poems convey is a proof of
the authenticity of the experience behind them. A mere
dreamer would surely imagine a tamer God, a mere
escapist a cosier retreat.

These poems explore mainly the lower—the purgatorial
with some glimpses of the illuminative—stages of the
mystic way. In the cancelled Preface to *New Poems* he
modestly disclaimed any higher intention. 'The first section
[which includes most of his best mystical poems] exhibits
mysticism in a limited and varying degree. I feel my
instrument yet too imperfect to profane by it the higher
ranges.' *Any Saint* is, perhaps, the only one which attempts
to enter these higher ranges, to suggest something of the
nature of the *Union*.

(ii) Some Poems

Arab Love-Song

The hunchèd camels of the night
Trouble the bright
And silver waters of the moon.
The Maiden of the Morn will soon
Through Heaven stray and sing,
Star-gathering.

Now while the dark about our loves is strewn,
Light of my dark, blood of my heart, O come!
And night will catch her breath up, and be dumb.

Leave thy father, leave thy mother
And thy brother;
Leave the black tents of thy tribe apart!
Am I not thy father and thy brother,
And thy mother?
And thou—what needest with thy tribe's black tents
Who hast the red pavilion of my heart?

This is one of the most deservedly famous of Thompson's poems, and here at least he achieves the maximum effect by the most economical means. The opening lines set the scene in a few words, conjuring up the atmosphere of night, the East, of mystery and beauty and expectancy. The image of the hunched camels (for cloud shapes) links up with the last line of the poem; for the red pavilion referred to is the small tent, lined inside with red, in which women rode on the backs of camels. The girl is to be taken to the heart of her lover, and within that she will be secure; at the same time one sees a picture of her within the red-lined tent on his camel.

The poem is quite satisfying as a simple love-song, but, following Father Connolly, I am sure that there is a second level of meaning beneath the obvious one. The first six lines of the final section are reminiscent of the passages in the Gospels (*Mark* X, 28-30; *Matthew* XII, 50) in which Christ calls on His followers to leave parents and brethren for His sake. So the lover here is, as well as the Arab, Christ, who calls the soul (always feminine to God in Thompson and other mystical writers) to leave the black tents of sin and come to the love and protection of the Sacred Heart. Looking back to the earlier parts of the poem we see that the images there are consonant with this interpretation, though they would not by themselves suggest it. The night under whose cover the lovers are to meet before the dawning is also the night of this life, in which the soul must give itself to Christ before the dawning of Eternity. In both cases there is a sense of urgency in the call to the beloved. It is significant that the dawn is not here spoken of with any hostility as it is in most night love poems.

Thompson's frequent association of the moon with the Virgin Mary may also be significant here; in the night of this life Mary the mediatrix helps the soul to find Christ, just as in the physical night the moon guides the lovers to their meeting.

In this apparently simple poem there is considerable density of meaning. The images work well together, and they work well on both levels of significance.

The bulk of Thompson's poetry consists of longish poems, mostly odes written in no regular stanza form. The lack of a tight metrical pattern allows him to sprawl, but on the other hand enables him to achieve some of his most characteristic effects. The sections into which they are divided and the poems as wholes are seldom firmly enough constructed; but as one gets to know the poems better one usually comes to see a more definite progression of thought and feeling and a greater density of meaning than one at first suspected.

The Hound of Heaven is the greatest of these Odes. Here we have a single great theme and a clear progression of feeling to give unity to the whole; and the sections, though some are too long, are given some shape by the refrain.

The theme, of course, is God's pursuit of man—an unusual one in modern religious verse, which more commonly deals with man's fumbling search for God. The poem has a wonderful speed and urgency, expressing in its rhythms the restlessness of the soul's flight and the majestic instancy of God's pursuit. Criticism of details may seem niggling in face of the power with which it brings to the imagination a sense of the presence of the supernatural as alive and active. Very few, especially modern, religious poems do anything like this; most make us feel in contact only with the author, who tells us what he did, thought, felt, etc., not with any power outside him. Nevertheless, even here some of Thompson's weaknesses as well as his greatness are displayed.

At first reading there may seem to be some needless repetition and turning back in the first three sections, which deal with the poet's flight from the love of God, which seems to make too great claims upon him. He seeks refuge in the thoughts and emotions of his own mind, in human love, in external nature, in children, and then (in the latter part of the third section) returns to nature. Why this return? On examination one sees that the two passages on nature are not repetitive, but deal with different experiences, presumably with different periods of the poet's life. In the first (when quite young?) he delighted in the power and beauty of nature and felt in himself something of the same vitality, but did not imagine natural things as sympathising with his emotions; the winds swept by unheeding. Later (perhaps when he became a poet?) he began to imagine a response from nature, sentimentally to cultivate the pathetic fallacy:

> I triumphed and I saddened with all weather
> Heaven and I wept together,
> And its sweet tears were salt with mortal mine.

His failing as a poet is that when he expresses such a weak mood, even if only to transcend it later, he tends to let the standard of the writing drop, as in:

> Let me twine with you caresses
> Wantoning
> With our Lady-Mother's vagrant tresses,
> Banqueting
> With her in her wind-walled palace, . . .

A greater poet would have been able to inject an undercurrent of irony under the sentimentality, so as to prepare us for the rejection of it in the stronger lines:

> For ah! we know not what each other says,
> These things and I; in sound *I* speak—
> *Their* sound is but their stir, they speak by silences.

And, having reached this point, a greater poet would not have relapsed into the rather infantile:

> Nature, poor stepdame, cannot slake my drouth;
> Let her, if she would owe me,
> Drop yon blue bosom-veil of sky, and show me
> The breasts o' her tenderness.

At the beginning of the fourth section the turning point is reached:

> Naked I wait Thy Love's uplifted stroke!

After this we may expect the poem to proceed rapidly to its conclusion; and we may be puzzled to find that nothing decisive happens for more than another forty lines, until we reach:

> That Voice is round me like a bursting sea.

The uplifted stroke of Love seems to remain suspended for an inordinate length of time; and during this time the protagonist is in a state of even greater depression than before. In the lines:

> And now my heart is as a broken fount
> Wherein tear-drippings stagnate . . .

he seems to have slipped back into an unpleasing self-pity. One has a sense of anti-climax. All this becomes intelligible, however, once one grasps that there are not just two, but three major stages in the protagonist's progress. In the first he flees from God and vainly seeks satisfaction in other things. In the second he no longer actively flees, but does not yet accept the love of God with any joy; his old life has been destroyed, but he has not yet entered upon a new; he realizes his own nothingness before God, but still apprehends Him primarily as the jealous God, who has deprived him of what he had wanted. This part culminates in the impressive vision:

> I dimly guess what Time in mists confounds;
> Yet ever and anon a trumpet sounds
> From the hid battlements of Eternity;
> Those shaken mists a space unsettle, then
> Round the half-glimpsèd turrets slowly wash again.
> But not ere him who summoneth
> I first have seen, enwound
> With glooming robes purpureal, cypress-crowned.

Is this figure just physical death, or death to self, or Christ in His Passion? Perhaps one does not need to choose. It is a vision of death seen as being necessary for the production of harvest, both in man's heart (where death to self is the kind of death demanded) and in life in general. The figure is primarily death rather than Christ, but its majesty and its presence on the battlements of Eternity suggest the idea that God Himself in Christ has accepted the principle which it embodies. The feeling behind the lines is still fearful rather than joyous, but the petulant complaint of the lines before has been worked through. The vision enables the poet to see his sufferings in perspective, and so to accept them. This leads on to the third stage, in which he inwardly surrenders and sees that he will find in God all that he previously sought elsewhere; fear yields to love. The writing in the last three sections is impressively simple and strong.

One sees, then, that there is a clear line of development in the poem. The weaknesses present, both spiritual and literary, are contained in a context in which they are transcended.

The difficult *The Mistress of Vision* is placed in the prominent first position in Thompson's best volume, *New Poems*. It is intentionally a fantasy, and has a lulling, dreamy rhythm. The meaning, of course, must be felt, and cannot be fully explained, but a discussion of some of the images may help towards feeling them more accurately. The Mistress of Vision sits at the heart of a secret garden, walled round with emerald; Life is its Warden, and it is to be reached only by passing over the fosse of Death. Father Connolly[1] says that the garden has a threefold significance; it is Heaven, the state of sinlessness on earth, and the realm of poetic achievement. Life, then, is Eternal Life in Heaven, the life of grace on earth and the life of the worthy poet; and Death is physical death, death to self and the particular death to self demanded by the poet's vocation. To the garden come birds (souls) and hang in air, enchanted by the singing of the Lady (primarily the Virgin Mary). In her song she prays:

> That the bowers might stay,
> Birds bate their winging,
> Nor the wall of emerald float in wreathèd haze away.

That is, that the garden may be preserved and that the souls may find permanent rest there. Here Father Connolly's first meaning does not quite apply, since there could be no question of the walls of Heaven dissolving away nor of souls who have once reached it ever departing. Here the garden seems to be a sort of paradisal state reached in moments of vision, but one in which there is as yet no secure abode.

The garden is lit by the light of the sun (Christ), which is low in the sky (reference to the Incarnation?), and in particular the Lady's body is aureoled and interstrewn with

[1] In the notes to his edition of Thompson's poems.

light. Mary is the perfection of sensible nature and as such the reflection (she is referred to as the moon) of the divine. But the Lady is, as well as Mary, the Muse, the inspirer of poetry; her words apply to the religious life, and also, more specifically, to the life of the poet and his means of attaining to that state of vision (the garden) out of which great poetry can arise. The garden includes the meanings Father Connolly sees in it, but it evokes also a whole complex of feelings connected with Eden, the lost Paradise, the Golden Age. It is the lost Eden to which in some special moments we seem to come home. The lady and the garden are archetypal images, which Thompson interprets in terms of his beliefs without banishing from them an indefinable richness of suggestion.

The first nine stanzas describe the Lady and the garden; in the rest of the poem Thompson tries to reconstruct what he can dimly remember of the Lady's song; but he knows that his own song is but a pale reflection of hers. (One is reminded here of that other visionary poem, *Kubla Khan*, which Coleridge breaks off with an implied confession of his inability to revive within him the song of the damsel with the dulcimer; Thompson, more boldly, presses on.) The burden of the Lady's song is the necessity, both for man and poet, of accepting suffering, and secondly of being able to see how all things are linked:

> When to the new eyes of thee
> All things by immortal power,
> Near or far,
> Hiddenly
> To each other linkèd are,
> That thou canst not stir a flower
> Without troubling of a star;
> When thy song is shield and mirror
> To the fair snake-curlèd Pain,
> Where thou dar'st affront her terror
> That on her thou may'st attain
> Perséan conquest; seek no more,
> O seek no more!
> Pass the gates of Luthany, tread the region Elenore.

The poem here turns upon itself and rebukes the mood of escapism which it itself in parts expresses and induces:

> Where is the land of Luthany
> And where the region Elenore?
> I do faint therefore.

The facile alliteration, the rather precious sound of 'Luthany' and 'Elenore', the word 'faint' all suggest a day-dreamy mood of desire to escape from the troubles of life into some cosy retreat; but the answer from the garden is an astringent reminder that entry to it is to be attained by acceptance of pain and by a new innocence of vision reached by discipline. So this poem, like others of Thompson, contains both escapist dreaming and real insight.

Other long Odes which are worth careful reading are *From the Night of Forebeing*, *Orient Ode* and *An Anthem of Earth*. The first of these deals with the times of dryness and unproductiveness in the spiritual life, compared with the similar periods of preparation before the flowering in the natural world (winter preluding spring) and in the whole plan of the creation (death as a prelude to rebirth, the cosmos arising out of chaos, the life of Heaven being prepared for in the life of earth). The themes are well combined so as to illuminate each other. *Orient Ode* is a hymn to the sun—as the physical sun, as an emblem of Christ and as Apollo, God of poetry. The sun is to the earth as Christ is to the soul, bringing to fruition the seeds of beauty which are contained in her. This emblematic way of looking at the natural world links Thompson with the medieval and metaphysical poets. Like them, he would say that he was not inventing conceits, but showing correspondences between different levels of being, correspondences which really exist. He makes much use of symbolism which is older than Christianity— deliberately, for, he says, 'primitive symbolism is really the recognition of a system of analogy inherent in the divine plan of the universe. All creation being an image of God, everything in man and nature is constructed on an identical plan, and one Divine analogy runs through all.' *Orient Ode* is shorter, more concentrated and better constructed than the earlier poem on a similar theme, *Ode to the Setting Sun*. A close study of the two would demonstrate Thompson's development.

Some of these Odes are too long; and some of the sections are lacking in definite shape. But they are not lacking in thought. They do not usually have an argumentive structure, proceeding from point to point in a chain of reasoning; and they do not usually show such a clear progression of feeling as *The Hound of Heaven*. They progress by unfolding the various meanings of an idea or symbol or group of symbols.

(iii) Diction

Thompson has been blamed for his 'passion for poly-syllables', his too consistently high-coloured language and his too frequent use of archaic, poetical and coined words. There is some justification for these criticisms. His language is apt to be as grandiose when writing of a poppy or of some trivial event as of the largest subjects. Sometimes this is deliberate, when he is showing how great things are contained in small; but sometimes it is due to a sort of automatism. When not inspired by strong feeling or deep thought his writing seems turgid and verbose. Further, he is sometimes too concerned about the sound of words to the neglect of immediate intelligibility. Some of his best lines are those in which he uses simple and short words.

Nevertheless I believe that the objection to Thompson's language is partly due to a prejudice which we ought to try to remove from our minds—a modern prejudice against poetic diction as such. Much of the greatest poetry in the world has been written in a language different from the current language of prose. The idea that poetry ought to be as like prose or ordinary speech as possible is not a primitive and natural, but a sophisticated and modern one. Of course in periods when there was an accepted convention of poetic diction it was much easier than it has been recently for a poet to write in a high style without seeming odd. The trouble with using a more 'poetical' diction than is customary is that it tends at first to draw the reader's attention to itself; the reader is puzzled, perhaps annoyed, perhaps delighted, by the words themselves, which may therefore to a certain extent stand between him and the meaning instead of revealing it. But it is not fair to judge by first impressions only. The test is whether, as one gets to know a poet's work better, the words become more luminous, come to seem more and more the fitting expression of the author's personality and of what he intends to convey. A careful reader of Thompson will, I believe, find this happening—at any rate, with many of the poems— as he begins to feel his way into Thompson's world. One of the reasons for the dislike of Thompson's diction is failure to read him with enough care, failure to appreciate the density of meaning which his words often contain.

It is certainly not true to say that Thompson was careless in his choice of words. He wrote: 'There are word-tasters and word-swillers. Unfortunately the two are confounded. Because the tasteless many among writers indulge in orgies of 'strong' and 'picturesque' language unrecking of fitness and delicate adjustment of meaning, a hue and cry goes out against the few whose love of language goes down to the sensitive roots of words, the few who never bang on a strong word like a tin kettle to deafen the ears of the groundlings, but use it because it is the exact vehicle for a strong thing; because it is not *a* strong word, but *the* strong word culled carefully from many strong words.' He used a special diction for a special purpose. He wrote: 'Essays dealing with subtle thoughts, like books dealing with scientific subjects, cannot be precisely expressed without the use of a specialised language, that is to say from the point of view of the man in the street. His language is too narrow and limited for their purpsoe—and, in another sense,

not limited enough. That is, it is too vague and imprecise.'
His aim was to express precisely a special content, to use
the strong word. The state of his MSS confirms that he
worked hard at his writing. It was his habit to write alterna-
tive versions of words and phrases above or below the
words he first wrote down; in many cases there are five or
six variants for a single word. In the MSS I have seen less
than half the lines were written straight out without
variants in the first draft and remained unaltered through
the often numerous revisions to the final version.

To say that he chose carefully and with purpose is not,
of course, to say that he always chose well. A fair judgement
could be reached only by an extensive and detailed examination of his words, for which there is not space here. He
was verbally inventive—coining words and making new
compounds, reviving archaic words, using noun for verb,
etc. The following are a few examples, with the words I
would draw attention to italicized:

> And so you said
> Things sweet *immeditatably* and wise.
>
> *Wintered* of sunning song
>
> Now with wan ray that other sun of Song
> Sets in the *bleakening* waters of my soul.
>
> The passing shower that rainbows *maniple*
>
> Music that is too *grievous* of the height
>
> Ill is *statured* to its opposite
>
> The *abashless* inquisition of each star
>
> She turned, with the *rout* of her dusk South hair
>
> While in a *moted* trouble the vexed gnats
> *Maze*, and vibrate, and tease the noontide hush.

The following are examples of original hyphenated com-
binations in Thompson—*wood-browned* pools, a *greening-*

sapphire sea, the *snow-cloistered* penance of the seed, *wind-besomed* chambers of the air.

All the above are attempts, variously successful, to express an exact meaning in a concentrated way. *Maniple*, for instance, is rather obscure, but full of meaning once understood. Normally a noun, it is used as a verb here. It is an ecclesiastical vestment like a small stole which hangs from the priest's left arm and which was originally used by the celebrant at Mass to wipe away tears or perspiration. 'Manipulus' is a sheaf; hence a symbol of joy. The rainbow appearing against the black cloud like a thin stole makes of the passing shower a maniple, a symbol of joy. The word not only expresses the idea of joy being associated with the acceptance of passing, of death and with tears and penitence, but also brings together the pageant of nature and ecclesiastical ritual—appropriately in the context (in *Ode to the Setting Sun*). On the other hand many passages could be quoted (parts of *Sister Songs*, for instance) where the unusual words are, at best, merely decorative. There are examples both of preciosity and of verbal invention to express precise and concentrated meanings in most of Thompson's poems. The task of criticism is to distinguish between the two, not to condemn the unusual or the 'poetical' as such.

In considering Thompson's use of words one should not think only of his oddities. He was capable of concentrated plain statement and of making good use of short and ordinary words—as in *Arab Love Song*, for instance. He quite often effectively puts a single long word in the midst of short ones, as in:

> I fled Him, down the nights and down the days;
> I fled Him, down the arches of the years;
> I fled Him, down the *labyrinthine* ways
> Of my own mind.

A similar good effect is obtained by the single longish words among the monosyllables in the first stanza of *The Kingdom of God*:

> O world invisible, we view thee,
> O world intangible, we touch thee,
> O world unknowable, we know thee,
> Inapprehensible, we clutch thee!

This skilful and restrained use of long words can be contrasted with the absurdity of, for instance, the description in *Sister Songs* of the evening sun shining on the child Sylvia:

> . . . sinking day, which, pouring its abundance
> Sublimed the illuminous and volute redundance
> Of locks . . .

Thompson's search for concentration, for density of meaning is seen in his frequent construction of adjectives in -ed from nouns. In the first twenty lines of *The Hound of Heaven* we find *vistaed* hopes, *chasmed* fears and *hearted* casement. This last phrase is rich in meaning in its context:

> I pleaded, outlaw-wise
> By many a hearted casement, curtained red.

One can understand this as a window shaped like a heart, and see the poet knocking outside the window, pleading to be admitted into the intimacy of the house; or one may think of the window of the heart itself, the heart of another person into which he wants to enter for refuge. It is the advantage of poetical over logical language that one does not need to choose between the two meanings, but can accept both.

IV: PROSE

There is space to deal only very briefly with Thompson's prose writings. They can be divided into three groups.

(i) Essays in poetic prose, written during his first few years as a writer. These are written in a mannered, rhythmical, metaphorical style, and include *Shelley* and *Moestitiae*

Encomium. They are, unfortunately, the best known of his prose works, but make up but a small proportion of his total output.

(ii) Books etc., on religious subjects. His short life of John Baptist de la Salle was composed—one supposes, hastily—for a special number of *Merry England* in 1891. It is written for the most part in a plain, undistinguished style, but breaks into eloquence in the final chapter, in which Thompson welcomes the increased concern for social justice to be found in his day, especially in his own Church. By the time of writing his other two religious works—a pamphlet, *Health and Holiness* (1905), and a full-scale life of Saint Ignatius Loyola, written, probably, at almost the same time—he had found a mean in style between undistinguished plainness and excessive elaboration. The biography of St. Ignatius is a compilation, based on secondary sources, but shows a poet's imagination at work in bringing events and people to life.

(iii) Journalism. In a notebook he wrote:

> 1897. End of Poet. Beginning of Journalist.
> The years of transition completed.

Before this he had contributed only a few articles and reviews to periodicals; for the last ten years of his life he was to make his living as a regular reviewer. Father Connolly has brought together about two hundred of his previously uncollected reviews and articles in *Literary Criticisms of Francis Thompson* (1948) and *The Real Robert Louis Stevenson and other critical essays* (1959). These are impressive volumes, displaying the wide range of Thompson's knowledge of literature, his sanity, his intelligence, his humour. The prose is consistently good, always lucid, sometimes eloquent and seldom too ornate for the purpose in hand. Anyone who wants to get a quick view of the quality of Thompson's mind would do well to turn to the last three of the reviews grouped under the heading *Mysticism: Genuine and Spurious* in the first of the above-mentioned collections. Thompson writes with great authority and precision on a subject which often leads to woolly thinking and inflated writing.

No one who reads much of Thompson's later prose could ever dismiss him as a fool or a mere neurotic dreamer.

V: CONCLUSION

One takes poems apart to look at words and images, but in the end it is the total effect of the poems as wholes, of the poet's works as a whole, that matters. Every writer has strengths and weaknesses, and one should be aware of both; but one's final opinion is not arrived at by coldly subtracting points against from points for. A major writer's fire seems to burn up the chaff; and I believe Thompson was a major writer—a great flawed writer, much more interesting and valuable than lesser ones of more even quality. If one were to demand artistic perfection, one would have to discard nearly all his poems, and might be left with only one or two short ones. In so doing one would have to cast out much that is of great value. He himself wrote of the ill effects of the cult of perfection: 'Over the whole contemporary mind is the trail of the serpent perfection . . . It leads in poetry to the love of minute finish, and *that* in turn (because minute finish is most completely attainable in short poems) leads to the tyranny of sonnet, ballade, rondeau, triolet and their kind. The principle leads again to aestheticism, which is simply the aspiration for a hot-house seclusion of beauty in a world which Nature has tempered by bracing gusts of ugliness.' (*The Way of Imperfection*). Later in the same essay he goes on: 'Critics have erected the ideal of a style stripped of everything special or peculiar, a style which should be to thought what light is to the sun. Now this pure white light of style is as impossible as undesirable; it must be splintered into colour by the refracting media of the individual mind, and humanity will always prefer the colour. Theoretically we ought to have no mannerisms; practically we cannot help having them, and without them style would be flavourless . . . We should avoid as far as possible the mannerisms of our age, because they corrupt originality. But in essence mannerisms—individual mannerisms, are a season of style, and happily unavoidable.' Thompson did not altogether avoid the mannerisms of his own, and earlier ages; sometimes his mannerisms are derivative, and corrupt originality; but more often they are the natural expression of his personality and vision. Few of his poems could possibly have been written by any one else, and few are without fine things in them.

So I end with a confession rather than an attempt at judicial summing up. For me Thompson's poems—in bulk, not just in a small selection—open new horizons, give a sense of exhilaration, and enhance the feeling of wonder.

FRANCIS THOMPSON

A Select Bibliography

(Place of publication London, unless stated otherwise)

Bibliography:

BIBLIOGRAPHIES OF MODERN AUTHORS (Second Series), by C. A. and H. W. Stonehill (1925)

—includes a bibliography of Francis Thompson's books.

ACCOUNT OF BOOKS AND MANUSCRIPTS OF FRANCIS THOMPSON, edited by T. L. Connolly. Boston (1937).

Note: Comprehensive bibliographies are contained in Rev. T. L. Connolly's edition of Thompson's Poems and (more complete and up-to-date) in M. P. Danchin's *Francis Thompson*.

Bibliographies of Thompson's reviews and literary criticism in periodicals are contained in Rev. T. L. Connolly's *Literary Criticisms by Francis Thompson* and *The Real Robert Louis Stevenson*.

The Oxford Standard Authors edition of Thompson's Poems has an appendix showing when and where the poems were first published.

Collected Editions:

SELECTED POEMS (1908)

—with a biographical note by W. Meynell.

WORKS [edited by W. Meynell] 3 vols. [1913]

—Vols. I and II contain all the poems Meynell considered worth preserving; Vol. III comprises a selection of his prose, mostly early work.

POEMS, edited by T. L. Connolly. New York (1932)

—revised edition, New York, 1941.

POEMS, Oxford (1937)

—the Oxford Standard Authors edition.

Separate Works:

THE LIFE AND LABOURS OF SAINT JOHN BAPTIST DE LA SALLE [1891].

—originally published in *Merry England;* revised edition, 1911.

POEMS (1893).

SISTER SONGS: AN OFFERING TO TWO SISTERS (1895)

—also privately printed, 1895, as *Songs Wing to Wing.*

NEW POEMS (1897).

VICTORIAN ODE FOR JUBILEE DAY, 1897 (1897)

—privately printed.

HEALTH AND HOLINESS (1905). *Prose*

—with a Preface by G. Tyrrell. Included in Vol. III of the *Works*.

SHELLEY (1909). *Prose*

—with an Introduction by G. Wyndham. Included in Vol. III of the *Works*.

SAINT IGNATIUS LOYALA, edited by J. H. Pollen (1909).   *Prose*.

A RENEGADE POET AND OTHER ESSAYS. Boston (1910). *Prose*

—with an Introduction by J. O'Brien.

UNCOLLECTED VERSE (1917)

—privately printed.

LITERARY CRITICISMS NEWLY DISCOVERED AND COLLECTED, edited by T. L. Connolly. New York (1948). *Prose*.

MINOR POETS BY FRANCIS THOMPSON, edited by T. L. Connolly. Los Angeles (1949)

—reprints of reviews by Francis Thompson.

THE MAN HAS WINGS, edited by T. L. Connolly. New York (1957)

—including hitherto unpublished poems and plays.

THE REAL ROBERT LOUIS STEVENSON AND OTHER CRITICAL ESSAYS, edited by T. L. Connolly. New York (1959)

—includes some uncollected articles and reviews by Thompson.

Some Biographical and Critical Studies:

THE LIFE OF FRANCIS THOMPSON, by E. Meynell (1913)

—a sympathetic but not uncritical biography by one who knew the poet well. Reprinted 1926.

DRAMATIS PERSONAE, by A. Symons (1925).

FRANCIS THOMPSON, THE POET OF EARTH IN HEAVEN, by R. L. Mégroz (1927)

—enthusiastic, rather uncritical, but interesting.

FRANCIS THOMPSON AND HIS POETRY, by T. H. Wright (1927).

FRANCIS THOMPSON AND WILFRED MEYNELL, A MEMOIR, by V. Meynell (1952)

—an excellent account, by W. Meynell's daughter, of the friendship of the two men. Contains new material.

FRANCIS THOMPSON, MAN AND POET, by J. C. Reid (1959)

—an interesting critical study.

FRANCIS THOMPSON: LA VIE ET L'OEUVRE D'UN POÈTE, par P. Danchin. Paris (1959)

—the most thorough and learned account of Thompson's life and work.